Everything You Need to Know About

Stress

Everyone experiences stress, but there are steps you can take to keep from pulling your hair out.

Everything You Need to Know About Stress

Eleanor H. Ayer

The Rosen Publishing Group, Inc.
New York

Published in 1994, 1998, 2001 by The Rosen Publishing Group, Inc.
29 East 21st Street, New York, NY 10010

Revised Edition 2001

Library of Congress Cataloging-in-Publication Data

Ayer, Eleanor H.
Everything you need to know about stress/Eleanor H. Ayer.
p. cm.
Includes bibliographical references and index.
ISBN 0-8239-3467-5
1. Stress (Psychology)—Juvenile literature. 2. Stress management—Juvenile literature. [1. Stress (Psychology). 2. Stress
management.] I. Title.
BF575.S75A94 1994
155.9'042—dc20
        94-434
        CIP
        AC

Manufactured in the United States of America

Contents

Introduction

Which of the following would you consider to be a stressful situation?

- Waiting to get picked for a team in gym class
- Waiting to be asked to the prom or planning to ask someone
- Getting an acceptance letter from your first-choice college
- Standing up in front of a class to deliver an oral report
- Being invited by a really popular student to the biggest party of the school year
- Being snubbed by a former best friend who now hangs out with a different crowd

◎ Beginning to date someone you've liked for a long time

◎ Walking toward the starting line before a track race

◎ Studying for a final exam in your least favorite subject

◎ Moving to a bigger, nicer house in a different neighborhood of the same town

◎ Winning your race for class president

Believe it or not, these are all highly stressful situations. A lot of people think stress is always related to bad or unpleasant things that make you angry, sad, or scared. But stress can also be caused by events that make you really happy, excited, or hopeful. Anytime your body experiences a rush of energy, whether it is caused by anger, sadness, excitement, or joy, it is under stress.

Occasional moments of stress aren't always a bad thing. The temporary energy burst stress provides can help you ace a difficult test, deliver a speech with infectious enthusiasm, hand your research paper in on time, or work up the nerve to ask someone out on a date. As long as the stress is short-term and the energy it generates is released, there is nothing to worry about. If you feel anxious on a daily basis,

Stress is not always bad. It can provide the energy you need to do well on tests.

however, so that your body is always in a state of tension and never feels any release, then stress has become a serious problem. You need to learn how to manage it before it begins to seriously affect your physical and emotional health.

Any change in your life, good or bad, can cause stress. Change, even for the better, is a threat because it creates a fear of the unknown. Moving to a bigger house in a nicer neighborhood, beginning to date someone you have liked for a long time, or getting into the college of your choice are all happy changes. But they are very stressful ones, too. Just as negative situations are perceived by our bodies as a threat to our emotional health, so are positive developments. Anything that threatens to change the lives that we know and are familiar with can generate stress.

Obviously, then, stress is just a fact of life—a natural and permanent part of our existence. We can never make it disappear entirely, nor should we; we need that survival instinct and its energy boost. Stress can be managed and put to good uses. This book will explain many of the causes of stress, the effects of stress on people, and ways to handle stress. Although stress will always be a part of your life, it doesn't have to be the biggest part of it.

Chapter 1

You Can Learn to Manage Stress

Do you ever convince yourself that you can't do something without even trying first? This is a form of stress. You are afraid of failure, and this fear keeps you from doing things that you might like and be very good at. One of the best ways to keep stress from taking over is to have high self-esteem. Having good self-esteem means believing in yourself. It means having the confidence to work through the stress and nervous feelings you have about something, and do it anyway.

Different people are stressed by different things. While you may be afraid to try new things for fear of failing, your best friend may become stressed out if she feels she isn't participating in enough activities. She may make herself too busy with athletics, school clubs, committees, student politics, and family commitments. As a result, she may often feel overwhelmed and spread too thin. There's not enough time in the day to complete all her work, so she feels a constant level of anxiety.

How stressful your life is depends on how you react to pressure. If you learn to control the way you react, you can learn to manage stress. Then stress will work for you rather than against you. It will help you become a more productive person.

There are many different ways to manage stress. What works for one person may not work for another, but each of us can learn to do it.

Ten Quick and Easy Tips to Reduce Stress

1. Balance your diet. Avoid stimulants such as caffeine, sugar, and nicotine, which give you a brief burst of energy but very quickly leave you feeling more tired and down than before. Never try to "take the edge off" with alcohol or drugs; these will only leave your body weaker and more stressed, and you may develop an addiction. Eat high-energy and nutritious foods, including grains, meat, and dairy products. Fruits and vegetables, in

particular, provide a natural energy and mood boost.

2. Get regular aerobic exercise (walking, jogging, swimming, biking, etc.). This will allow your body to release the "bad" energy of stress that makes you feel ill if it is not burned off. Exercise will also boost your immune system, energy level, and mood.

3. Relax! Try to schedule regular relaxation breaks throughout your day. Set aside time for reading, listening to music, or meditation. Be sure to get plenty of rest and try to stick to a regular sleep schedule.

4. Breathe deeply. Whenever you have a free moment, take a few deep breaths. Breathe in deeply through your nose, hold the breath for a few moments, then release it. Let your body go slack. You'll actually feel the stress and tension leaving your body!

5. Smile! Keep smiling, even when confronting things that make you

mad, sad, or scared. Try to find the humor in things, even those things that are causing you stress. Don't avoid or bury your problems, but approach them with a good sense of humor, if possible.

6. Avoid negativity. Whenever possible, avoid the company of people who are always negative. Negativity is contagious and poisonous. Try to help your friends and family members who are sad, depressed, or angry, but don't get swept along by their moods. Every time you find yourself thinking negatively, force yourself to find a positive way to look at the same situation.

7. Stay positive. Remember that what comes around goes around. If you make an effort to be positive and treat others with kindness and compassion, you will most likely receive the same treatment from others. Creating a positive climate around you will help buffer you against stress.

8. Take control. Even though you cannot always control what happens to you, you can control how you react to the unexpected stressful events in your life. Treat these situations as challenging problems to be solved. This enthusiastic, "can do" approach will help make you feel that you can deal with any stressful situation that may arise.

9. Talk about it. Studies have shown that people who don't have friends or family members to talk to about their problems have much higher levels of stress. It's no accident that married people live longer than single people. So don't feel you must go it alone. Share your worries with people you trust. They will give you a different perspective, some good advice, and the strength to face your fears. Most important, they will allow you to blow off steam.

10. Reward yourself. Treat yourself to a movie, a new CD or book, or just some time off after you've worked hard and completed a good job.

Chapter 2

Preventing Stress-Related Illness

People are not born with "high-stress" or "low-stress" personalities. But some people are at a higher risk for stress than others. Read the following statements and think about whether they apply to you.

⊙ I get frustrated and then angry very easily.

⊙ I'm never the best at anything. Someone can always do it better.

⊙ I've always been the best at everything I do. I can't stand the thought of not being the best, but I'm worried that I won't be able to keep it up for much longer.

⊙ I feel responsible for the happiness of my friends and family.

If not handled wisely, stress can cause people to behave irrationally and even violently.

- I have too many commitments: school-work, athletics, after-school activities, my part-time job, friends, and family.

- I feel like no one wants to hang out with me. I'm the person everyone forgets to call.

- I often feel depressed.

- Other people come to me with their problems and looking for advice, but no one asks how I'm doing. I don't have anyone to talk to.

- I worry all the time, even about things that I can't do anything about or that haven't even happened yet and may never happen.

- I have been through a major life change in the past year (switched schools, moved to a new town, parents divorced, close relative died, illness of family member, new sibling born, etc.).

If any of these statements apply to you, you may be suffering from the effects of long-term stress. Even if you're at risk for stress, however, you can learn how to manage it.

Stress and Illness

Doctors believe that there is a link between stress and illness. In fact, the American College of Physicians estimates that 80 percent of the people who visit doctors' offices have stress-related ailments. Some doctors put this estimate as high as 90 percent. Forty-five percent of adults have experienced stress-related illness, whether they have sought treatment for it or not. Stress has been linked to most of the leading causes of death, including heart disease, cancer, lung diseases, accidents, and suicide.

Eating a healthy diet full of fruits and vegetables can help you manage and prevent stress.

People who are easily stressed are more likely to get sick than the average person. Headaches, insomnia (having trouble falling or staying asleep), lack of energy, body aches, skin rashes, colds, the flu, less resistance to infection, stomachaches, cold sores, accidental injury, loss of interest in favorite activities, and a loss or increase in appetite are all possible reactions to stress.

The effects of stress don't stop there, however. People who suffer stress for a long period of time are at a higher risk for developing diabetes, cancer, arthritis, asthma, heart disease, heart attacks, high blood pressure, ulcers, panic attacks, strokes, abuse of alcohol or drugs, and depression. You will never have a stress-free life, but you must learn how to manage stress before it kills you!

A Healthy Diet

Stress squeezes the energy out of your body. Eating a healthy diet is a good way to help manage stress and replace lost nutrients. Not just any food will replenish you and soothe your nerves. In fact, some foods increase your chances of feeling stress. Foods that have caffeine or a lot of sugar can cause hyperactivity in some people. Hyperactivity is a state of nervousness that makes it hard for a person to sit still and concentrate. It's true that the stimulants caffeine, sugar, and nicotine can give you a brief boost of energy and a feeling of well-being, but these effects don't last long at all. Within minutes of the "rush," you will crash, ending up at a lower energy level than where you started.

A better way to derive energy from sugar is to eat cereals, rice, pasta, bread, and potatoes. These foods contain natural sugars that are released into your blood more slowly than sugar found in chocolate, candy, donuts, cola, or sweetened coffee. As a result, the sugar level in your blood remains more stable, and you avoid sugar "highs" and "lows."

Among the best stress-reducing foods are fresh fruits and vegetables. It's thought that they can help boost your brain's natural "feel good" chemicals, improving your mood and energy level. Fruits and vegetables should be part of a well-balanced diet that also includes grains, meat, and dairy products. To really cover your bases, you can also take a multivitamin and mineral supplement.

So put down that chocolate bar, pour out that soda, and stub out that cigarette. Have a salad. Drink some juice. Snack on a banana. You'll start feeling more relaxed and energetic almost immediately!

Get Regular Rest

Being overtired only makes matters worse. To help reduce stress, it's important to go to bed and get up at about the same time every day. This helps keep your body's inner "clock" running smoothly. If you are overtired and have an irregular sleep schedule, this clock gets out of whack. The result is that production of your brain's natural feel-good chemicals—those chemicals that fight stress, regulate your body temperature, let you enjoy a deep, restful sleep, boost your energy, relieve pain, and increase pleasure—goes way down.

Chapter 3

How to Tell When You're "Stressed Out"

What are the warning signs of stress? There are many different ways to spot stress. Not all stress sufferers will have all of these signs, but they will have some of them.

◎ Headache, chest and back pain, dizziness, and an overall feeling of weakness

◎ Upset stomach, hiccups, and diarrhea

◎ Tightness or twitching of muscles

◎ Grinding of teeth

◎ Frequent illness or complaints about pain

◎ Nail biting, hair pulling, or similar behavior

◎ Weakened immune system

- Changes in sleeping or eating habits
- Constant fatigue, irritability, anger, or anxiety
- Memory lapses and problems concentrating and sitting still
- Depression, loss of self-confidence, and low self-esteem
- High blood pressure
- Ulcers
- Anxiety attacks

Fight or Flight: An Ancient Instinct in Modern Times

Even though it often seems like stress is something new, something that didn't exist before cell phones, traffic jams, divorce, drug abuse, guns in schools, and busy schedules began complicating our families' lives, it is actually as old as the very first human being. While most of our stress is caused by non-life-threatening annoyances and anxieties, primitive humans worried about survival every day of their very short lives. While we struggle with the fear of losing a game, being dumped by a boyfriend or girlfriend, or failing a test, our earliest ancestors faced a daily fight for life against starvation, severe weather, and savage animals.

In order to cope with these terrors, evolution provided primitive humans with an early form of stress management: the fight-or-flight response. When confronted with a life-threatening situation, our ancestors, listening to their instincts, could either stay and fight or run away and hopefully live to fight another day. In order to be able to fight or flee, the body needed a burst of energy, a jolt of adrenaline, to prepare for whatever challenges lay ahead. That energy is stress, and it is the body's way of preparing itself for an exhausting battle or escape.

Human lives have changed drastically since then, but in some ways evolution hasn't caught up yet. Modern

Responding to stress with a flight reaction can cause self-destructive behaviors, such as alcohol abuse.

humans still experience the fight-or-flight response, often on a daily basis, even though the dangers we are fighting and fleeing from are very different now. With the technological and medical advances of modern life, most of us face far fewer life-threatening situations. Our bodies, however, are still programmed to identify dangers and react to them with bursts of energy—stress. We start taking faster, shorter breaths. Our hearts beat much more rapidly. We may get an adrenaline rush. Our livers send more energy-providing sugar into our blood. Our blood pressure goes way up, filling our muscles with the blood, nutrients, and oxygen we will need to fight or flee. This is the exact same physical reaction that our ancestors experienced when confronted with a hungry lion or a violent storm.

What stresses us out today, however, tends to be threats to our emotional, rather than physical, health. This is why you get butterflies in your stomach before playing a soccer game you fear you may lose, cry when a friend starts to ignore you, or become angry when someone else gets the lead in the school play. These situations are all threatening to your peace of mind and the life that you want to create for yourself. So your body reacts with these strong emotions in an attempt to get you through the momentary crisis. Just as in primitive times, you can choose to deal with these situations directly (fighting) or avoid them (fleeing), depending on what seems best for you at that moment.

The Modern Fight Reaction

Many times a fight reaction is violent. But violence is not the only way to resist. There are many kinds of fight reactions. You may have used some yourself.

- ◎ Arguing, rudeness, temper tantrums, bullying, teasing
- ◎ Defying authority
- ◎ Aggressive, dangerous behavior, such as reckless driving or playing with guns
- ◎ Stealing or cheating

The Modern Flight Reaction

Some people are born "fighters." Others just want to run away when things get tense. Here are some ways that young people often "take flight."

◎ Sleep for long periods of time

◎ Withdraw, become quiet

◎ Work extremely long and hard at a job or project

◎ Act in self-destructive ways (smoking, drinking, using drugs, and engaging in risky sexual activity)

◎ Lie about or blame others for one's actions

◎ Eat too much or starve oneself

◎ Stay away from home for long periods of time

Chapter 4

Learning About Stressors

A stressor is a cause of stress, something that is threatening to a person. This can be a physical or mental condition, an event, another person, or the person himself or herself. We all have little irritations that bring us distress, such as being in the slowest checkout line in a store. But stressors are the cause of ongoing, long-term stress, the kind that doesn't go away overnight.

Stressors Change As We Change

Our stressors change as we get older. Preschool children are often afraid of the dark, which makes bedtime stressful. A first grader may be shy and afraid to leave home. For her or him, going to school is stressful.

There are many general types of stressors in a teen's life. Some of the more common stressors are:

◎ Families—Arguments with brothers, sisters, parents, stepparents

◎ School—Pressure to get good grades, obeying the rules, respecting authority, avoiding potentially dangerous situations, such as those involving drugs or weapons

◎ Peers—Fitting in, forming close friendships, boyfriend/girlfriend relationships, peer pressure to try drugs or alcohol or engage in sexual activity

◎ Changing bodies—Sexual development, changes in height, weight, body shape, and self-image

Sometimes our stressors are very serious, life-changing events. Studies show that the following can be the most critical stressors in a teenager's life:

◎ Your parents separate or divorce

◎ A divorced parent remarries

◎ A parent, sibling, or close friend dies

◎ One or both parents lose a job

◎ You move to a new house or a new town

◎ You go to a new school

- ◎ You learn that you are pregnant (and you are an unmarried girl)

- ◎ You learn that you are going to be a father (and you are an unmarried boy)

- ◎ You break up with your boyfriend or girlfriend

- ◎ You have a brush with the law

- ◎ You or a close friend starts using drugs or alcohol

- ◎ You discover that you are adopted

If any of these events have happened to you during the past year, you are probably living under great stress. You've probably been sick more often than usual. You may feel tired constantly. You may be having trouble eating and sleeping. Your stomach or head always seems to ache. You're probably moody and sometimes overjoyed or depressed, but rarely in between. It doesn't help that, as an adolescent, your hormones are also in a period of tremendous change, making your mood swings even more extreme. Just realize that this is all perfectly normal, and if you recognize that these are the effects of stress, you can set about trying to reduce your stress levels. These are major events that make permanent changes in your life; it's no wonder you feel stressed out!

Talking about your problems with a trusted adult can help relieve stress in your life.

But it doesn't always take such drastic events to bring on stress. Lesser events can also be the cause of major stress. You are probably living under stress if you have had one or more of the following things happen to you recently.

◎ **A change in the way your friends feel about you, either good or bad**

◎ **People are gossiping about you**

◎ **You begin dating, or your friends begin dating and you don't**

◎ **A sibling is born or adopted**

- A sibling moves out of the house
- You have no one to talk to about your problems, worries, and joys
- Too many or too few social obligations
- Working a part-time job while in school
- Too little sleep
- Trying to get into college or going away to college

In a sense, your body doesn't care whether you are experiencing major life-changing events or more common daily developments. It just knows that your stressors, dramatic or not, are wearing you down. Your body reacts in the exact same way to all stress—great and small—so you should do the same. Be energetic in attempting to reduce your stress, no matter what is causing it.

You May Be Your Own Worst Stressor

We often think that our stress is caused by things outside of ourselves. We see ourselves as innocent victims of the pressures and demands of the world. Sometimes, however, the stress we feel starts within us and causes negative things to happen (for example, spending all of your paycheck on CDs will result in your not being able to afford to go to a concert with your friends). Or at the very least, the way we deal with life's stress can sometimes just make things worse and increase our anxiety. It is no one's fault but your own if you take on more duties and activities than you can possibly accomplish. Do you really need to be treasurer of the photography club, varsity soccer captain, class vice president, yearbook editor, and part-time bookstore clerk all at the same time? Learn to prioritize and zero in on the things you most want to do.

It's also no one's fault but your own if you have to pull an all-nighter before an exam that was announced a month ago but which you hadn't started studying for until after dinner. Try to manage your time wisely so that you don't waste large blocks of time procrastinating and doing nothing and then find yourself scrambling to finish something that requires a lot of work in a very short period.

Even if the stress you feel is caused by something that is beyond your control—like a divorce or a move to a new town—you can take responsibility for the way you react to this stress. This will allow you to feel in control again. Just be careful how you go about trying to reduce the stress. Don't try to reduce it by avoiding it or "smoothing it over" with drugs or alcohol. This will just push your problems out of sight where they will grow as the pressure increases. Soon you'll be like a volcano ready to explode, and your body will be more exhausted and in pain than it was before you partied. Using drugs or alcohol is never a solution. It only increases your problems.

Face your stressors head-on by talking about your feelings with someone you trust. This will help you blow off a lot of steam. If you can't change the stressful situation, see if you can change your attitude toward it by looking on the bright side ("Maybe my parents will be happier now that they're divorced, and maybe I'll get along better with them"; "I might meet some great new people in this town, and my old friends aren't so far away that I can't see them often"). And always remember to exercise and eat right; release that bad energy and generate some good energy!

Realistic Ideas

Another source of stress is living with unrealistic ideas about life. Do you have any of these ideas?

Perfectionism. You set impossibly high standards for yourself and become stressed when you realize you can't live up to them. Try to remember that you can't be the greatest at everything you do. Take some pressure off yourself by focusing on those things you really like to do and are interested in (whether you're good at them or not). Then set realistic goals for achievement. Most important, enjoy yourself!

Low self-esteem. You are sure that you are going to fail at whatever you try even before you start. This kind of attitude can become a self-fulfilling prophecy, which means you will indeed fail, but not because you lack talent; you fail because you convince yourself that you are a failure. If thinking that you are a failure can make you fail, then the opposite is equally true. Start telling yourself that you'll be just fine. You'll do your best job, and, while it may not be perfect, it will be pretty good. And you'll keep working at it and keep improving. This shift in attitude can make all the difference in reducing your fear of failure and can lead to real success. Remember, everyone fails once in a while, even geniuses, star athletes, politicians, musicians, and movie stars. Failure and the attempt to improve are what make us human.

Controlling. People who feel the need to be in control of everything that affects their lives are often suffering under an enormous amount of stress. It's important to make peace with the fact that we just can't control everything that happens to us. All we can control is how we deal with those things. We also have no control over the way other people think or act. We can't force other people to like us or agree with us or do what we want them to do. All we can do is try to be the best people we can be and hope that our good attitude encourages others to like us and share our ideas. Realizing you have only limited control over a situation and loosening your grip can be scary, but it can also make you feel much lighter and more free.

Chapter 5

Reducing Stress by Changing Your Behavior

Doing what it takes to reduce stress in your life does not require a degree in psychology or medicine. You know your body and the way it feels better than anyone else ever could. If it starts telling you it is under too much stress, you'll hear it loud and clear. Then it is time to do something about the stress that is affecting your mood and health. Reducing stress isn't a very complicated process. It just requires that you follow some commonsense guidelines, adopt more healthy lifestyle choices, and make a few hard decisions about what you should cut out of your life.

Get Organized

Disorganization can be a major source of stress. There are few things more aggravating than looking for something that you need but have misplaced. If you don't have enough time to search for it thoroughly, your anxiety and annoyance will only increase. If this happens to you on a regular basis, you are placing yourself under a heavy load of unnecessary stress.

It may seem like a lot of work to take the time to straighten up, putting your clothes, books, keys, and papers in their proper places. The few minutes you spend doing this every day, however, will almost certainly take less time than your daily frantic searches. Just by knowing exactly where to find the things you need, you will go a long way toward reducing your daily stress levels.

Be a Good Time Manager

One of the greatest sources of stress is having too much to do in too little time. You may have three term papers to write and four final exams to study for in one week. Or you may have a long list of chores to finish around the house before you can go out on Saturday night. This creates a sense that you are drowning in work, and that overwhelmed feeling is extremely stressful. Sometimes it can be so overwhelming that you don't know where to begin and have trouble completing any one of your tasks.

Study after study has shown that people whose lives are filled with many time-consuming tasks have much higher stress levels than those who are

Learning to reduce your workload and to manage your time more efficiently can go a long way toward reducing your stress load.

less busy. This is no surprise. But what can you do to reduce this stress?

The best approach is a combination of reducing the number of things you have to do and using the time you do have more efficiently. When you wake up in the morning, make a list of all the things you hope to get done that day. Once everything is written down, go through the list and remove anything that doesn't seem necessary or can wait until tomorrow. Once you have a final list of the things that must get done, organize them in time slots, being sure to allow plenty of time for the completion of each job. If you don't allow yourself enough time for each task, you will find yourself scrambling to finish and falling behind your schedule, and your stress will only increase.

Be sure to build into this schedule some time for relaxation as well. This will allow you to recharge your batteries between tasks. Give yourself a half hour or so here and there for reading, socializing, TV watching, listening to music, or exercise.

Some More Dos and Don'ts

Don't try to be all things to all people. You can't be a star athlete, get straight As, hold down a job after school, volunteer at the local hospital, and be a friend to everyone in town. You're only one person. Others may admire you for trying to be a superteen, but they don't have to live with your stress. Be honest. Know when to say, "I have to slow down." Learning how to say no is one of life's most important but hardest lessons. Don't sacrifice your happiness and health just because you're afraid of hurting someone's feelings. When you say no to someone's request for your time, gently explain to him or her why you cannot help out or join him or her this time.

Think positively. People who see the dark side of everything are usually stress-prone. When an idea is suggested, they immediately think of reasons why it won't work. Negative thinkers tend to be depressed. They are afraid to take risks that will improve their lives because they feel that their lives are out of their control.

On the other hand, think about the people you know who are always "up" and live each day to the fullest. They have confidence in themselves and in their ability to control their lives. If they should fail at something, their world does not come to an end. They accept their mistakes and try to learn from them. Generally, a positive person has a good sense of humor, which is a great help in relieving the tension that can lead to stress.

Chapter

6

Mind over Matter

Ari Kiev is a psychiatrist and author of many books on mental health, including *A Strategy for Daily Living.* In his practice, he works with teenagers suffering from stress and depression. He says that reducing stress depends on how you handle a situation. "It may be unpleasant for you to hear that the problem is in your hands," he warns. "But if you learn to control your reactions, situations that once seemed impossible will begin to look like challenges, not obstacles."

Sure, you say, that may be true. But how do I learn to control my reactions? How do I turn an obstacle into a challenge?

You're in Charge

Start by telling yourself, "It's up to me. I'm in charge here." Don't look for someone to blame for your stress. Don't look for someone to help you out of it. Rely on yourself.

"Other people and events and things do not stress you," says Dr. M. W. Buckalew, who teaches classes on stress management. "*You* stress you." In his book *Learning to Control Stress*, Dr. Buckalew says that if you talk properly to yourself, you will not get angry as often. You will start to see things in a different way. Here are some ways to help you reduce your stress by changing your perspective.

Take responsibility for what has happened. Say "I made myself so mad," not "He made me so mad."

Don't label yourself. Stop calling yourself shy, clumsy, or stupid. Instead, talk about your behavior. "That decision I made was really dumb," not "I'm so dumb." Or "During the game my dribbling was clumsy," instead of "I'm so clumsy."

Be sure to give yourself positive affirmation. Tell yourself "I can do this," "I can reach my goals," "I'll take this one step at a time," "I've been through worse," "I'm a great person and I just have to keep being myself," "I learn from my mistakes," "I've just done a great job."

Don't set yourself up for failure. It's good to have high ideals. But don't set goals that are impossible to meet. You'll quickly become frustrated. The frustration will lead to a lack of self-confidence.

Welcome change. Change can often be very scary, but there's no sense in resisting it. It will come whether you want it to or not. So try to think of upcoming changes as exciting, even if scary. Change brings new opportunities and may make you feel reenergized and more interested in what's going on around you.

Imagining Success

How do you prepare to handle a stressful situation? You can "rehearse" for a stressful event, such as a speech, party, or college interview, by imagining it in detail ahead of time. Start by imagining the event running smoothly. Think of how you will act, what might be asked of you, how you will respond to expected questions, conversations, or activities.

Then imagine several variations. Imagine what unexpected things may occur, what minor problems could crop up. Think about how you will react to these unforeseen circumstances. By imagining an event and its likely flow and possible snags, you will feel more prepared for it, less uncertain of what it will involve, and more ready to deal with any surprises. When the big day finally comes, you will feel almost as if you have done it before, and your anxiety will be that much lower.

Using Your Brain to Break the Tension

Here are some other ways to use your head to change your attitude, solve your problems, and reduce stress.

Psych up. Get excited about an event that you expect to be stressful. Instead of worrying about it, look forward to it. Tell yourself that even if it will make you nervous, it will also be a fun and interesting new experience. Focus on this, and don't let the fear of stress prevent you from doing what you really want to do.

Stay calm. At first this may seem unnatural, like you're putting on an act. But the longer you put on that act, the more natural it becomes. By acting calm, you can convince both your body and your mind that you are calm.

Take a break. Sometimes the best way to relieve stress is to walk away for a little while. Change the scene. In a different place, your stressor may suddenly seem much less important. The broader perspective you gain by temporarily leaving your problems behind and walking around the wider world may make that fight with your friend or the impossible math problem seem much smaller and more manageable. By taking time to blow off steam and distract yourself with other thoughts, you can often return to problems refreshed and suddenly find the solution very quickly.

Finish tasks. Often we invite stress by never finishing what we start. We think of ourselves as failures because we don't accomplish our goals, even the simple ones. Break the stress by getting out your chore chart and doing at least two of those jobs— right now! This will create some momentum to help you finish other tasks, and you'll feel greatly relieved.

Write it down! Writing is a great form of stress relief. Keep a journal or write a letter to yourself when you get frustrated or upset. Explain what has upset you, why you think it has upset you, and what you can do to either solve the problem or at least feel better about the situation. Try also to write down something that made you happy or thankful that day.

Be kind. Say or do something nice for someone else today. Not only will you be making someone else feel good (which is reason enough to do it), but it will make you feel good about yourself, too. Your positive self-image will help reduce stress in your life, and people will be more drawn to you. Plus, acts of kindness are often like a boomerang; they have a way of coming back to help you just when you need it.

Chapter 7
Physical Ways to Relieve Stress

As important as it is to reduce stress by changing the way you think about your problems, you will always feel some level of stress every day. And this stress will collect in your body and begin to have bad effects on your health. It is absolutely necessary to allow your body to release this stress by slowing your heart rate, controlling your breathing, lowering your blood pressure, and relaxing your muscles.

The Importance of Deep Breathing

Deep breathing is a common relaxation technique, one that many cultures have practiced for thousands of years as a necessary first step to spiritual enlightenment. Taking a few deep breaths at various times throughout the day is a great way to become instantly more relaxed.

You can do it anywhere and anytime: after the alarm clock wakes you up, after you get out of the shower, just before walking into school, while waiting on the lunch line, on the bus ride home, or just before you go to sleep.

Begin by closing your eyes. Let your body go limp. Close your mouth and breathe deeply through your nose until it feels like your lungs can't hold any more air. Hold the breath for several seconds and then slowly release it. You can repeat this several times in one session, but don't overdue it; you may begin to hyperventilate.

Can't you already feel the tension flowing out of your body? Just one deep breath will make your heart slow down, your blood pressure decrease, and your blood become more filled with energizing oxygen. Taking several deep breathing breaks during your busy day is a far better way to release stress and gain energy than a junk food binge or coffee break.

Training Your Body to Relax

Meditation is another excellent way to relieve stress. To do it, you must sit still and concentrate very hard. You want to try to focus all your thoughts on just one relaxing or pleasant thing for a certain amount of time (twenty to thirty minutes is ideal). This allows you to temporarily stop thinking about the problems that are causing you stress. As a result, your body will relax, and by the end of your meditation session, you will feel refreshed and more optimistic and calm. You will also be carrying around far less stress in your body.

Find a comfortable position in a quiet room. Lying on the floor on your back works well. Begin by taking a few deep breaths, holding them, and releasing them slowly. Then focus on something simple, like the rhythm of your own heartbeat, a physical object that pleases you (flowers, a candle flame, a painting, or a photo), or the silent repetition of a word or sound. You can also visualize a beautiful and soothing place in your mind and imagine you are there. Or you can imagine good health and relaxation entering your body with each breath you take, and illness and tension leaving with each breath you release. Whatever technique you use, it is important to block out all other sights, sounds, and troubling thoughts or distractions. If you notice that worries are creeping into your thoughts, ignore them and refocus on your one pleasurable sound, image, or object. Soon your body will begin to relax. A soothing feeling will wash over you.

Progressive Muscle Relaxation

One of the most common effects of stress on your body is tense muscles. Muscles that become tight in your back and neck can lead to serious backaches and headaches. When your body is in pain, you can become even more stressed, which means your body can become even more tight and painful. It's a vicious cycle.

One way to break the cycle is to practice progressive muscle relaxation. This involves first tensing your muscles for five seconds and then letting them go slack and releasing all tension. By tensing the muscles first, the feeling of relief is greater when you let them relax. Sit in a comfortable chair or lie down on a bed or the floor. Close your eyes and focus on the parts of your body that feel especially tense. There are fifteen muscle groups you should tense and relax. Tense and release each of these groups of muscles in the following order: right hand and forearm; right bicep; left hand and forearm; left bicep; forehead; cheeks and nose; mouth; neck and shoulders; chest and stomach; right thigh; right foot and calf; right toes; left thigh; left foot and calf; left toes.

After each tensing, enjoy the feeling of relaxation that follows. Focus on the tension that is leaving your body. When you have completed tensing and releasing each muscle group, lie or sit still for a few minutes to bask in the new stillness and relaxation. Take several deep breaths to complete the process and prepare yourself to return to your busy life.

You can also use muscle relaxation at any time during the day to concentrate on specific areas of tension. If you feel like your neck and shoulders are tightening up, take a moment to relax those muscles. You may be able to prevent the onset of a stress headache this way.

Working Off Stress Through Exercise

Exercise is perhaps the best stress reduction technique of all. Stress generates a lot of energy in your body even as it makes you feel drained (remember, your body is gearing up for a fight or flight). If that energy isn't released, it can cause serious health problems. Exercise reverses the process by helping your body let go of that pent-up energy while also making you feel more energized.

Setting a regular exercise time each day helps to reduce stress in many ways. People who exercise regularly have an easier time keeping weight off. Their cholesterol levels, muscle tone, and flexibility all improve. It gives a boost to your immune system, allowing you to better fight off diseases, infections, viruses, and the effects of stress. Exercise even makes it easier to quit smoking and overeating. Exercise helps to increase blood flow to your brain, bringing it sugars and oxygen that you need in order to think clearly and work hard. This increased blood flow also removes toxins in your brain that collect and make it hard for you to concentrate and solve problems. Exercise causes the release of the brain's feel-good chemicals that act as natural painkillers and mood enhancers. A good workout also helps you to sleep longer and more deeply. Finally, exercise gets the body in shape for handling

long-term stress, the kind that doesn't go away when your temper cools down.

There are many ways to relieve stress through exercise. You can run, swim, jump rope, play tennis, or just walk. Exercise helps loosen up your muscles. As we've just seen, when your muscles are relaxed, stress is relieved. Exercise also helps focus your attention on something other than your stressor. When you're concentrating on a tennis ball, for example, you forget how upset you are with your girl-friend or boyfriend. When you're jogging or walking, the change of scenery helps you forget your problems at home.

Be sure to choose exercise that you like. Otherwise, the exercise time will only add more stress to your life. Remember, this doesn't have to be a bodybuilding program. It is a program to reduce stress. Best of all, you don't have to set aside a lot of time to get some real benefits from exercise. As few as three fifteen-minute sessions of exercise a week can begin to relieve your body of its burden of stress.

Other Physical Ways to Reduce Stress

◎ Take a nap

◎ Get a massage

◎ Take a hot bath

◎ Drink a glass of warm milk

◎ Listen to relaxation tapes of recorded nature sounds

Chapter 8

You're in Control

When you feel as though your life is crazy and you're completely stressed out, take a deep breath and say to yourself, "I'm in control."

You have the skills you need to manage the stress in your life. You just need to use them. Knowing your strengths and weaknesses, setting realistic goals, and establishing an outlet for your stress are all good ways to cope with stress.

Don't fall into the trap of "the easy out." These outs can include using drugs or alcohol, ignoring your responsibilities, or avoiding the people who cause you stress. These avoidance techniques will only make your stress and your life worse. You need to deal with your stressors head-on. You can't do this if you're drunk, high, or avoiding life.

Four attitudes can help you take control of your life.

There is good in every situation. Look for the good even in things that seem to be going bad. For example, maybe your mom and dad are fighting again, but you're going to spend the night at a friend's house, which is always a lot of fun. Finding the good will help you think positively, which will put you in a better frame of mind to manage your stress.

Things could be worse. Sometimes it helps to figure out just how they might be worse. Suzanne's parents were divorced. Suzanne was disappointed that she had to visit her dad on the weekend rather than going out with her friends. Then she thought about her friend Rosie. Rosie's dad left when Rosie was just a baby. She hasn't seen him since. Suzanne realized that she was lucky to be able to see her dad regularly. She pulled out her weekend bag and happily started packing.

Most problems have solutions. Stress sometimes builds because you can't see the answers to your problems. Things seem hopeless. But by having confidence in yourself and believing in yourself, you have the tools you need to take control and find a solution.

Time heals all wounds. No matter how bad things may be, no matter how great the stress, things will seem better after some time has passed. The stress you feel because of the death of a relative or a close friend may last for months. But once you have learned to manage the stress, you'll be able to focus on the positive things in your life once again.

Once you accept that stress will always be a part of your life, you can concentrate on your reactions to stress and stressors. Stress will take a backseat, and you will be ready to face life and all its challenges.

Glossary

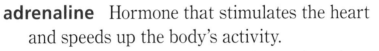

adrenaline Hormone that stimulates the heart and speeds up the body's activity.

alcohol A substance found in liquor that changes the way a person thinks and acts.

anxiety Feeling of worry or nervousness.

caffeine Stimulant found in coffee, chocolate, and other food items that excites the brain and nervous system.

confident Sure, certain, full of faith.

control A state of having power over a situation; to take responsibility for your actions.

depressed Overcome by a feeling of gloom or deep sadness.

distress State of pain, suffering, danger, or trouble.

exhaustion State of being extremely weak or tired.

fight-or-flight response The way the body reacts to stress by producing chemicals and sending messages to the brain that prepare a person to fight or run from the stressor.

hormones Chemicals in the glands that help the body grow, stay in balance, and react to outside stimulants.

hyperactivity More activity or movement than average.

irritable Impatient, angry; in a bad mood that makes one very sensitive.

meditation Mental exercise that focuses deeply on a single idea, thought, or object.

outcome The result of taking action.

progressive muscle relaxation The tensing and relaxing of muscles to help release stress.

self-confidence Trust or faith in oneself.

self-destructive Harmful to oneself.

self-esteem How a person feels about himself or herself.

stressed out Overcome by stress.

stressor A cause of stress.

tension Mental strain, worry; a feeling of being pulled in different directions.

Where to Go for Help

The first step in managing your stress is to let an adult know that you are having trouble. If your own parent cannot help, talk to a school counselor, social worker, religious leader, or a friend's parent.

If you think you may need more help, there are other places to look. Most communities have mental health centers, clinics, or hospitals that deal with stress-related problems. To find a clinic in your town or city, look in the yellow pages under Stress Management or Mental Health Services. Asking for help in managing your stress is not a sign of weakness. It is a sign of strength and courage. It means that you care enough to help yourself. The following is a list of some national organizations that deal with stress management.

In the United States

American Institute of Stress
124 Park Avenue
Yonkers, NY 10703
(914) 963-1200
e-mail: stress124@earthlink.net
Web site: http://www.stress.org

American Public Health Association (APHA)
800 I Street NW
Washington, DC 20001
(202) 777-2742
e-mail: comments@apha.org
Web site: http://www.apha.org

The Hardiness Institute, Inc.
4425 Jamboree, Suite 140
Newport Beach, CA 92660
(949) 252-0580
Web site: http://www.hardinessonline.com

The National Institute of Mental Health (NIMH)
6001 Executive Boulevard, Room 8184
MSC 9663

Bethesda, MD 20892-9663
(301) 443-4513
Web site: http://www.nimh.nih.gov

In Canada

The Canadian Institute of Stress
Medcan Clinic Office, Suite 1500
150 York Street
Toronto, ON M5H 3S5
(416) 236-4218
e-mail: earle@direct.com
Web site: http://www.stresscanada.org

Canadian Mental Health Association (CMHA)
2160 Yonge Street, Third Floor
Toronto, ON M4S 2Z3
(416) 484-7750
e-mail: cmhanat@interlog.com
Web site: http://www.cmha.ca

For Further Reading

Coleman, William L. *Teen Stress: Stories to Guide You.*
Minneapolis, MN: Augsburg Fortress, 1994.

Harris, Rachel. *20-Minute Retreats: Revive Your Spirit
in Just Minutes a Day with Simple Self-Led Practices.*
New York: Henry Holt and Company, 2000.

Kiev, Ari. *A Strategy for Daily Living: The Classic Guide
to Success and Fulfillment.* Rev. ed. New York: Free
Press, 1997.

McCoy, Kathy, and Charles Wibbelsman. *Life Happens.*
New York: Perigree, 1996.

Packard, Gwen K. *Coping with Stress.* New York: The
Rosen Publishing Group, Inc., 1997.

Saunders, Charmaine. *Teenage Stress.* Birch Grove,
Australia: Sally Milner Publishers, 1993.

Weil, Andrew. *Eating Well for Optimum Health: The
Essential Guide to Bringing Health and Pleasure
Back to Eating.* New York: Quill, 2001.

Index

About the Author

Eleanor H. Ayer is the author of several books for children and young adults. She has written about people of the American West, World War II and modern Europe, and current social issues of interest to teenagers. Her recent topics include depression, teen fatherhood, teen marriage, and teen suicide. Ms. Ayer holds a master's degree from Syracuse University with a specialty in literacy journalism. She lives with her husband and two sons in Colorado.

Photo Credits

Cover and p. 18 © Pictor; p. 2 © Ron Chapple/FPG; p. 8 © Owen Franken/Corbis; p. 16 © Index Stock; p. 23 © AP World Wide Photo; p. 24 by Antonio Mari; p. 30 © Telegraph Colour Library/FPG; p. 38 © Corbis; p. 51 © Vladimir Pcholkin/FPG.

Series Design

Thomas Forget

Layout

Les Kanturek

DATE DUE

			Printed in USA

HIGHSMITH #45230